What I Love About You, GRANDPA

Dear Grandpa:

I love you! This book is full of things I love about you. There might also be an exciting new vehicle in here, too.

Love,

_____

Grandpa, I love to

_____

_____

(activity you do together)

with you!

Here's a selfie of us:

(draw you & your grandpa doing the activity)

Grandpa, I love when you give me . . .

○ high fives

○ presents

○ candy

○ _____ !

Grandpa, you make me laugh when you

_____!

Grandpa, I love you even more than . . .

○ popsicles

○ Halloween

○ movies

○ _____ !

Good news, Grandpa!
I got you a . . .

O flying car!

O hot air balloon!

O pirate ship!

O _____ !

Grandpa, I have an idea!

Let's make a special holiday just for YOU.
We can play

_____

and eat

_____!

Doesn't that sound great?

Grandpa, I always think of you when _____.

Guess what else?
I think you would be a great . . .

○ chef
○ wizard
○ clown

○ _____ !

Grandpa, if you were an animal, you'd be . . .

○ an eagle

○ a tiger

○ a wolf

○ a bear

○ _____ !

(draw your grandpa as a cool animal!)

Grandpa, I think you have pretty interesting . . .

○ stories about when you were a kid
○ junk in your house
○ jokes

○ _____ !

(color this page for your grandpa!)

Grandpa, you deserve some awards.

OUTSTANDING ACHIEVEMENT IN THE FIELD OF

- ◯ Singing!
- ◯ Playing Games!
- ◯ Just Hanging Out!

◯ _____!

SUPER TOP-NOTCH

- ◯ Cook!
- ◯ Book Reader!

◯ _____!

Grandpa, I think the world would be a much better place if you were in charge of...

○ snacks
○ taking care of people
○ everything

○ _____!

Grandpa, I got you a crazy turtleneck!

Isn't it . . .

○ the best turtleneck you've ever seen?
○ cosmic?
○ so ugly it's AWESOME?

○ _____ ?

It made me feel . . .

◯ excited!
◯ grown-up!
◯ silly!

◯ _____ !

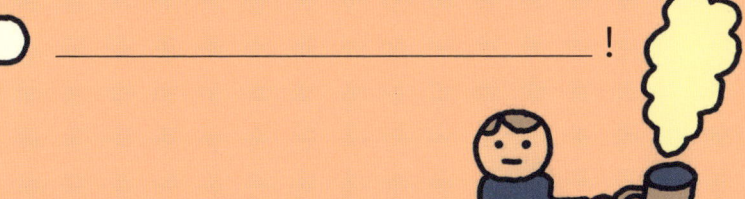

Grandpa, I think you are a . . .

- ⭕ decent
- ⭕ pretty excellent
- ⭕ COMPLETELY EPIC
- ⭕ _____

grandpa.

I give you

thumbs up!

(plus _____ hugs)
(write a big number here)

Grandpa, I love you so much I would probably even let you borrow my

_____!

Grandpa, someday I hope I can be as good as you at . . .

○ being funny
○ fixing stuff
○ giving advice

○ _____.

Grandpa, I would love to give you your very own . . .

○ aquarium
○ farm
○ water park

○ _____.

And maybe a lifetime supply of _____!

Grandpa, I feel

_____

_____

_____

that you are my grandpa,
and I am your grandkid!

I LOVE YOU, GRANDPA!

Love,

_____

PS: Could you get me a . . .

- ⭕ crocodile
- ⭕ sugar glider

- ⭕ _____

for my next birthday, please?

Created, published, and distributed by Knock Knock
6695 Green Valley Circle, #5167
Culver City, CA 90230
knockknockstuff.com
Knock Knock is a registered trademark of Knock Knock LLC
Fill in the Love is a registered trademark of Knock Knock LLC

© 2025 Knock Knock LLC
All rights reserved
Illustrations by Benoit Tardif
Made in China

No part of this product may be used or reproduced in any manner whatsoever without prior written permission from the publisher, except in the case of brief quotations embodied in critical articles and reviews. For information, address Knock Knock.

ISBN: 978-1-68349-565-9
UPC: 8-25703-11139-2

CC-06/2025-01

You Fill In The Love.®